Christopher Columbus
And The New World of His Discovery
Volume 8

FILSON YOUNG
[ZHINGOORA BOOKS]

About Author

Alexander Bell Filson Young was a journalist, BBC programme advisor and author. His wrote the book on Titanic, a RMS Titanic ship. His famous works includeTitanic, The Relief of Mafekingand etc.

CHAPTER VI

RELIEF OF THE ADMIRAL

There was no further difficulty about provisions, which were punctually brought by the natives on the old terms; but the familiar, spirit of sedition began to work again among the unhappy Spaniards, and once more a mutiny, led this time by the apothecary Bernardo, took form—the intention being to seize the remaining canoes and attempt to reach Espanola. This was the point at which matters had arrived, in March 1504, when as the twilight was falling one evening a cry was raised that there was a ship in sight; and presently a small caravel was seen standing in towards the shore. All ideas of mutiny were forgotten, and the crew assembled in joyful anticipation to await, as they thought, the coming of their deliverers. The caravel came on with the evening breeze; but while it was yet a long way off the shore it was seen to be lying to; a boat was lowered and rowed towards the harbour.

As the boat drew near Columbus could recognise in it Diego de Escobar, whom he remembered having condemned to death for his share in the rebellion of Roldan. He was not the man whom Columbus would have most wished to see at that moment. The boat came alongside the hulks, and a barrel of wine and a side of bacon, the sea-compliment customary on such occasions, was handed up. Greatly to the Admiral's surprise, however, Escobar did not come on board, but pushed his boat off and began to speak to Columbus from a little distance. He told him that Ovando was greatly distressed at the Admiral's misfortunes; that he had been much occupied by wars in Espanola, and had not been able to send a message to him before; that he greatly regretted he had no ship at present large enough to bring off the Admiral and his people, but that he would send one as soon as he had it. In the meantime the Admiral was to be assured that all his affairs in Espanola were being attended to faithfully, and that Escobar was instructed to bring back at once any letters which the Admiral might wish to write.

The coolness and unexpectedness of this message completely took away the breath of the unhappy Spaniards, who doubtless stood looking in bewilderment from Escobar to Columbus, unable to believe that the caravel had not been sent for their relief. Columbus, however, with a self-restraint which cannot be too highly praised, realised that Escobar meant what he said, and that by protesting against his action or trying to interfere with it he would only be putting himself in the wrong. He therefore retired immediately to his cabin and wrote a letter to Ovando, in which he drew a vivid picture of the distress of his people, reported the rebellion of the Porras brothers, and reminded Ovando that he relied upon the fulfilment of his promise to send relief. The letter was handed over to Escobar, who rowed back with it to his caravel and immediately sailed away with it into the night.

Before he could retire to commune with his own thoughts or to talk with his faithful brother, Columbus had the painful duty of speaking to his people, whose puzzled and disappointed faces must have cost him some extra pangs. He told them that he was quite satisfied with the message from Ovando, that it was a sign of kindness on his part thus to send them news in advance that relief was coming, that their situation was now known in San Domingo, and that vessels would soon be here to take them away. He added that he himself was so sure of these things that he had refused to go back with Escobar, but had preferred to remain with them and share their lot until relief should come. This had the desired effect of cheering the Spaniards; but it was far from representing the real sentiments of Columbus on the subject. The fact that Escobar had been chosen to convey this strange empty message of sympathy seemed to him suspicious, and with his profound distrust of Ovando Columbus began to wonder whether some further scheme might not be on foot to damage him in the eyes of the Sovereigns. He was convinced that Ovando had meant to let him starve on the island, and that the real purpose of Escobar's visit had been to find out what condition the Admiral was in, so that Ovando might know how to act. It is very hard to get at the truth of what these two men thought of each other. They were both suspicious, each was playing for his own hand, and Ovando was only a little more unscrupulous than Columbus; but there can be no doubt that whatever his motives may have been Ovando acted with abominable treachery and cruelty in leaving the Admiral unrelieved for nearly nine months.

Columbus now tried to make use of the visit of Escobar to restore to allegiance the band of rebels that were wandering about in the neighbourhood under the leadership of the Porras brothers. Why he should have wished to bring them back to the ships is not clear, for by all accounts he was very well rid of them; but probably his pride as a commander was hurt by the thought that half of his company had defied his authority and were in a state of mutiny. At any rate he sent out an ambassador to Porras, offering to receive the mutineers back without any punishment, and to give them a free passage to Espanola in the vessels which were shortly expected, if they would return to their allegiance with him.

The folly of this overture was made manifest by the treatment which it received. It was bad enough to make advances to the Porras brothers, but it was still worse to have those advances repulsed, and that is what happened. The Porras brothers, being themselves incapable of any single-mindedness, affected not to believe in the sincerity of the Admiral's offer; they feared that he was laying some kind of trap for them; moreover, they were doing very well in their lawless way, and living very comfortably on the natives; so they told Columbus's ambassadors that his offer was declined. At the same time they undertook to conduct themselves in an amicable and orderly manner on condition that, when the vessels arrived, one of them should be apportioned to the exclusive use of the mutineers; and that in the meantime the Admiral should share with them his store of provisions and trinkets, as theirs were exhausted.

This was the impertinent decision of the Porras brothers; but it did not quite commend itself to their followers, who were fearful of the possible results if they should persist in their mutinous conduct. They were very much afraid of being left behind in the island, and in any case, having attempted and failed in the main object of their mutiny, they saw no reason why they should refuse a free pardon. But the Porras brothers lied busily. They said that the Admiral was merely laying a trap in order to get them into his power, and that he would send them home to Spain in chains; and they even went so far as to assure their fellow-rebels that the story of a caravel having arrived was not really true; but that Columbus, who was an adept in the arts of necromancy, had really made his people believe that they had seen a caravel in the dusk; and that if one had really arrived it would not have gone away so suddenly, nor would the Admiral and his brother and son have failed to take their passage in it.

To consolidate the effect of these remarkable statements on the still wavering mutineers, the Porras brothers decided to commit them to an open act of violence which would successfully alienate them from the Admiral. They formed them, therefore, into an armed expedition, with the idea of seizing the stores remaining on the wreck and taking the Admiral personally. Columbus fortunately got news of this, as he nearly always did when there was treachery in the wind; and he sent Bartholomew to try to persuade them once more to return to their duty—a vain and foolish mission, the vanity and folly of which were fully apparent to Bartholomew. He duly set out upon it; but instead of mild words he took with him fifty armed men—the whole available able-bodied force, in fact—and drew near to the position occupied by the rebels.

The exhortation of the Porras brothers had meanwhile produced its effect, and it was decided that six of the strongest men among the mutineers should make for Bartholomew himself and try to capture or kill him. The fierce Adelantado, finding himself surrounded by six assailants, who seemed to be directing their whole effort against his life, swung his sword in a berserk rage and slashed about him, to such good purpose that four or five of his assailants soon lay round him killed or wounded. At this point Francisco de Porras rushed in and cleft the shield held by Bartholomew, severely wounding the hand that held it; but the sword. stuck in the shield, and while Porras was endeavouring to draw it out Bartholomew and some others closed upon him, and after a sharp struggle took him prisoner. The battle, which was a short one, had been meanwhile raging fiercely among the rest of the forces; but when the mutineers saw their leader taken prisoner, and many of their number lying dead or wounded, they scattered and fled, but not before Bartholomew's force had taken several prisoners. It was then found that, although the rebels had suffered heavily, none of Bartholomew's men were killed, and only one other besides himself was wounded. The next day the mutineers all came in to surrender, submitting an abject oath of allegiance; and Columbus, always strangely magnanimous to rebels and insurgents, pardoned them all with the exception of Francisco de Porras, who, one is glad to know, was confined in irons to be sent to Spain for trial.

This submission, which was due to the prompt action of Bartholomew rather than to the somewhat feeble diplomacy of the Admiral, took place on March 20th, and proved somewhat embarrassing to Columbus. He could put no faith in the oaths and protestations of the mutineers; and he was very doubtful about the wisdom of establishing them once more on the wrecks with the hitherto orderly remnant. He therefore divided them up into several bands, and placing each under the command of an officer whom he could trust, he supplied them with trinkets and despatched them to different parts of the island, for the purpose of collecting provisions and carrying on barter with the natives. By this means the last month or two of this most trying and exciting sojourn on the island of Jamaica were passed in some measure of peace; and towards the end of June it was brought to an end by the arrival of two caravels. One of them was the ship purchased by Diego Mendez out of the three which had arrived from Spain; and the other had been despatched by Ovando in deference, it is said, to public feeling in San Domingo, which had been so influenced by Mendez's account of the Admiral's heroic adventures that Ovando dared not neglect him any longer. Moreover, if it had ever been his hope that the Admiral would perish on the island of Jamaica, that hope was now doomed to frustration, and, as he was to be rescued in spite of all, Ovando no doubt thought that he might as well, for the sake of appearances, have a hand in the rescue.

The two caravels, laden with what was worth saving from the two abandoned hulks, and carrying what was left of the Admiral's company, sailed from Jamaica on June

28, 1504. Columbus's joy, as we may imagine, was deep and heartfelt. He said afterwards to Mendez that it was the happiest day of his life, for that he had never hoped to leave the place alive.

The mission of Mendez, then, had been successful, although he had had to wait for eight months to fulfil it. He himself, in accordance with Columbus's instructions, had gone to Spain in another caravel of the fleet out of which he had purchased the relieving ship; and as he passes out of our narrative we may now take our farewell of him. Among the many men employed in the Admiral's service no figure stands out so brightly as that of Diego Mendez; and his record, almost alone of those whose service of the Admiral earned them office and distinction, is unblotted by any stain of crime or treachery. He was as brave as a lion and as faithful as a dog, and throughout his life remained true to his ideal of service to the Admiral and his descendants. He was rewarded by King Ferdinand for his distinguished services, and allowed to bear a canoe on his coat-of-arms; he was with the Admiral at his death-bed at Valladolid, and when he himself came to die thirty years afterwards in the same place he made a will in which he incorporated a brief record of the events of the adventurous voyage in which he had borne the principal part, and also enshrined his devotion to the name and family of Columbus. His demands for himself were very modest, although there is reason to fear that they were never properly fulfilled. He was curiously anxious to be remembered chiefly by his plucky canoe voyage; and in giving directions for his tomb, and ordering that a stone should be placed over his remains, he wrote: "In the centre of the said stone let a canoe be carved, which is a piece of wood hollowed out in which the Indians navigate, because in such a boat I navigated three hundred leagues, and let some letters be placed above it saying: Canoa." The epitaph that he chose for himself was in the following sense:

Here lies the Honourable Gentleman

DIEGO MENDEZ

He greatly served the royal crown of Spain in
the discovery and conquest of the Indies with
the Admiral Don Christopher Columbus of
glorious memory who discovered them, and
afterwards by himself, with his own ships,
at his own expense.
He died, etc.
He begs from charity a PATERNOSTER
and an AVE MARIA.

Surely he deserves them, if ever an honourable gentleman did.

CHAPTER VII

THE HERITAGE OF HATRED

Although the journey from Jamaica to Espanola had been accomplished in four days by Mendez in his canoe, the caravels conveying the party rescued from Puerto Santa Gloria were seven weary weeks on this short voyage; a strong north-west wind combining with the west-going current to make their progress to the north-west impossible for weeks at a time. It was not until the 13th of August 1503 that they anchored in the harbour of San Domingo, and Columbus once more set foot, after an absence of more than two years, on the territory from the governorship of which he had been deposed.

He was well enough received by Ovando, who came down in state to meet him, lodged him in his own house, and saw that he was treated with the distinction suitable to his high station. The Spanish colony, moreover, seemed to have made something of a hero of Columbus during his long absence, and they received him with enthusiasm. But his satisfaction in being in San Domingo ended with that. He was constantly made to feel that it was Ovando and not he who was the ruler there;—and Ovando emphasised the difference between them by numerous acts of highhanded authority, some of them of a kind calculated to be extremely mortifying to the Admiral. Among these things he insisted upon releasing Porras, whom Columbus had confined in chains; and he talked of punishing those faithful followers of Columbus who had taken part in the battle between Bartholomew and the rebels, because in this fight some of the followers of Porras had been killed. Acts like these produced weary bickerings and arguments between Ovando and Columbus, unprofitable to them, unprofitable to us. The Admiral seems now to have relapsed into a condition in which he cared only for two things, his honours and his emoluments. Over every authoritative act of Ovando's there was a weary squabble between him and the Admiral, Ovando claiming his right of jurisdiction over the whole territory of the New World, including Jamaica, and Columbus insisting that by his commission and letters of authority he had been placed in sole charge of the members of his own expedition.

And then, as regards his emoluments, the Admiral considered himself (and not without justice) to have been treated most unfairly. By the extravagant terms of his original agreement he was, as we know, entitled to a share of all rents and dues, as well as of the gold collected; but it had been no one's business to collect these for him, and every one's business to neglect them. No one had cared; no one had kept

---

any accounts of what was due to the Admiral; he could not find out what had been paid and what had not been paid. He accused Ovando of having impeded his agent Carvajal in his duty of collecting the Admiral's revenues, and of disobeying the express orders of Queen Isabella in that matter; and so on-a state of affairs the most wearisome, sordid, and unprofitable in which any man could be involved.

And if Columbus turned his eyes from the office in San Domingo inland to that Paradise which he had entered twelve years before, what change and ruin, dreary, horrible and complete, did he not discover! The birds still sang, and the nights were still like May in Cordova; but upon that happy harmony the sound of piteous cries and shrieks had long since broken, and along and black December night of misery had spread its pall over the island. Wherever he went, Columbus found the same evidence of ruin and desolation. Where once innumerable handsome natives had thronged the forests and the villages, there were now silence and smoking ruin, and the few natives that he met were emaciated, terrified, dying. Did he reflect, I wonder, that some part of the responsibility of all this horror rested on him? That many a system of island government, the machinery of which was now fed by a steady stream of human lives, had been set going by him in ignorance, or greed of quick commercial returns? It is probable that he did not; for he now permanently regarded himself as a much-injured man, and was far too much occupied with his own wrongs to realise that they were as nothing compared with the monstrous stream of wrong and suffering that he had unwittingly sent flowing into the world.

In the island under Ovando's rule Columbus saw the logical results of his own original principles of government, which had recognised the right of the Christians to possess the persons and labours of the heathen natives. Las Casas, who was living in Espanola as a young priest at this time, and was destined by long residence there and in the West Indies to qualify himself as their first historian, saw what Columbus saw, and saw also the even worse things that happened in after years in Cuba and Jamaica; and it is to him that we owe our knowledge of the condition of island affairs at this time. The colonists whom Ovando had brought out had come very much in the spirit that in our own day characterised the rush to the north-western goldfields of America. They brought only the slightest equipment, and were no sooner landed at San Domingo than they set out into the island like so many picnic parties, being more careful to carry vessels in which to bring back the gold they were to find than proper provisions and equipment to support them in the labour of finding it. The roads, says Las Casas, swarmed like ant-hills with these adventurers rushing forth to the mines, which were about twenty-five miles distant from San Domingo; they were in the highest spirits, and they made it a kind of race as to who should get there first. They thought they had nothing to do but to pick up shining lumps of gold; and when they found that they had to dig and delve in the hard earth, and to dig systematically and continuously, with a great deal of digging for very little gold, their spirits fell. They were not used to dig; and it happened that most of them began in an unprofitable spot, where they digged for eight days without finding any gold. Their provisions were soon exhausted; and in a week they were back again in San Domingo, tired, famished, and bitterly disappointed. They had no genius for steady labour; most of them were virtually without means; and although they lived in San Domingo, on what they had as long as possible, they were soon starving there, and selling the clothes off their backs to procure food. Some of them took situations with the other settlers, more fell victims to the climate of the island and their own imprudences and distresses; and a thousand of them had died within two years.

Ovando had revived the enthusiasm for mining by two enactments. He reduced the share of discovered gold payable to the Crown, and he developed Columbus's system of forced labour to such an extent that the mines were entirely worked by it. To each Spaniard, whether mining or farming, so many natives were allotted. It was not called slavery; the natives were supposed to be paid a minute sum, and their employers were also expected to teach them the Christian religion. That was the plan. The way in which it worked was that, a body of native men being allotted to a Spanish settler for a period, say, of six or eight months—for the enactment was precise in putting a period to the term of slavery—the natives would be marched off, probably many days' journey from their homes and families, and set to work under a Spanish foreman. The work, as we have already seen, was infinitely harder than that to which they were accustomed; and most serious of all, it was done under conditions that took all the heart out of the labour. A man will toil in his own garden or in tilling his own land with interest and happiness, not counting the hours which he spends there; knowing in fact that his work is worth doing, because he is doing it for a good reason. But put the same man to work in a gang merely for the aggrandisement of some other over-man; and the heart and cheerfulness will soon die out of him.

It was so with these children of the sun. They were put to work ten times harder than any they had ever done before, and they were put to it under the lash. The light diet of their habit had been sufficient to support them in their former existence of happy idleness and dalliance, and they had not wanted anything more than their cassava bread and a little fish and fruit; now, however, they were put to work at a pressure which made a very different kind of feeding necessary to them, and this they did not get. Now and then a handful of pork would be divided among a dozen of them, but they were literally starved, and were accustomed to scramble like dogs for the bones that were thrown from the tables of the Spaniards, which bones they ground up and mixed with their, bread so that no portion of them might be lost. They died in numbers under these hard conditions, and, compared with their lives, their deaths must often have been happy. When the time came for them to go home they were generally utterly worn out and crippled, and had to face a long journey of many days with no food to support them but what they could get on the journey; and the roads were strewn with the dead bodies of those who fell by the way.

And far worse things happened to them than labour and exhaustion. It became the custom among the Spaniards to regard the lives of the natives as of far less value than those of the dogs that were sometimes set upon them in sport. A Spaniard riding along would make a wager with his fellow that he would cut the head off a native with one stroke of his sword; and many attempts would be laughingly made, and many living bodies hideously mutilated and destroyed, before the feat would be accomplished. Another sport was one similar to pigsticking as it is practised in India, except that instead of pigs native women and children were stuck with the lances. There was no kind of mutilation and monstrous cruelty that was not practised. If there be any powers of hell, they stalked at large through the forests and valleys of Espanola. Lust and bloody cruelty, of a kind not merely indescribable but unrealisable by sane men and women, drenched the once happy island with anguish and terror. And in payment for it the Spaniards undertook to teach the heathen the Christian religion.

The five chiefs who had ruled with justice and wisdom over the island of Espanola in the early days of Columbus were all dead, wiped out by the wave of wild death and cruelty that had swept over the island. The gentle Guacanagari, when he saw the desolation that was beginning to overwhelm human existence, had fled into the mountains, hiding his face in shame from the sons of men, and had miserably died there. Caonabo, Lord of the House of Gold, fiercest and bravest of them all, who first realised that the Spaniards were enemies to the native peace, after languishing in prison in the house of Columbus at Isabella for some time, had died in captivity during the voyage to Spain. Anacaona his wife, the Bloom of the Gold, that brave and beautiful woman, whose admiration of the Spaniards had by their bloody cruelties been turned into detestation, had been shamefully betrayed and ignominiously hanged. Behechio, her brother, the only cacique who did not sue for peace after the first conquest of the island by Christopher and Bartholomew Columbus, was dead long ago of wounds and sorrow. Guarionex, the Lord of the Vega Real, who had once been friendly enough, who had danced to the Spanish pipe and learned the Paternoster and Ave Maria, and whose progress in conversion to

Christianity the seduction of his wives by those who were converting him had interrupted, after wandering in the mountains of Ciguay had been imprisoned in chains, and drowned in the hurricane of June 30, 1502.

The fifth chief, Cotabanama, Lord of the province of Higua, made the last stand against Ovando in defence of the native right to existence, and was only defeated after severe battles and dreadful slaughters. His territory was among the mountains, and his last insurrection was caused, as so many others had been, by the intolerable conduct of the Spaniards towards the wives and daughters of the Indians. Collecting all his warriors, Cotabanama attacked the Spanish posts in his neighbourhood. At every engagement his troops were defeated and dispersed, but only to collect again, fight again with even greater fury, be defeated and dispersed again, and rally again against the Spaniards. They literally fought to the death. After every battle the Spaniards made a massacre of all the natives they could find, old men, children, and pregnant women being alike put to the sword or burned in their houses. When their companions fell beside them, instead of being frightened they became more furious; and when they were wounded they would pluck the arrows out of their bodies and hurl them back at the Spaniards, falling dead in the very act. After one such severe defeat and massacre the natives scattered for many months, hiding among the mountains and trying to collect and succour their decimated families; but the Spaniards, who with their dogs grew skilful at tracking the Indians and found it pleasant sport, came upon them in the places of refuge where little groups of them were sheltering their women and children, and there slowly and cruelly slaughtered them, often with the addition of tortures and torments in order to induce them to reveal the whereabouts of other bands. When it was possible the Spaniards sometimes hanged thirteen of them in a row in commemoration of their Blessed Saviour and the Twelve Apostles; and while they were hanging, and before they had quite died, they would hack at them with their swords in order to test the edge of the steel. At the last stand, when the fierceness and bitterness of the contest rose to a height on both sides, Cotabanama was captured and a plan made to broil him slowly to death; but for some reason this plan was not carried out, and the brave chief was taken to San Domingo and publicly hanged like a thief.

After that there was never any more resistance; it was simply a case of extermination, which the Spaniards easily accomplished by cutting of the heads of women as they passed by, and impaling infants and little children on their lances as they rode through the villages. Thus, in the twelve years since the discovery of Columbus, between half a million and a million natives, perished; and as the Spanish colonisation spread afterwards from island to island, and the banner of civilisation

14

and Christianity was borne farther abroad throughout the Indies, the same hideous process was continued. In Cuba, in Jamaica, throughout the Antilles, the cross and the sword, the whip-lash and the Gospel advanced together; wherever the Host was consecrated, hideous cries of agony and suffering broke forth; until happily, in the fulness of time, the dire business was complete, and the whole of the people who had inhabited this garden of the world were exterminated and their blood and race wiped from the face of the earth . . . . Unless, indeed, blood and race and hatred be imperishable things; unless the faithful Earth that bred and reared the race still keeps in her soil, and in the waving branches of the trees and the green grasses, the sacred essences of its blood and hatred; unless in the full cycle of Time, when that suffering flesh and blood shall have gone through all the changes of substance and condition, from corruption and dust through flowers and grasses and trees and animals back into the living body of mankind again, it shall one day rise up terribly to avenge that horror of the past. Unless Earth and Time remember, O Children of the Sun! for men have forgotten, and on the soil of your Paradise the African negro, learned in the vices of Europe, erects his monstrous effigy of civilisation and his grotesque mockery of freedom; unless it be through his brutish body, into which the blood and hatred with which the soil of Espanola was soaked have now passed, that they shall dreadfully strike at the world again.

CHAPTER VIII

THE ADMIRAL COMES HOME

On September 12, 1504., Christopher Columbus did many things for the last time. He who had so often occupied himself in ports and harbours with the fitting out of ships and preparations for a voyage now completed at San Domingo the simple preparations for the last voyage he was to take. The ship he had come in from Jamaica had been refitted and placed under the command of Bartholomew, and he had bought another small caravel in which he and his son were to sail. For the last time he superintended those details of fitting out and provisioning which were now so familiar to him; for the last time he walked in the streets of San Domingo and mingled with the direful activities of his colony; he looked his last upon the place where the vital scenes of his life had been set, for the last time weighed anchor, and took his last farewell of the seas and islands of his discovery. A little steadfast looking, a little straining of the eyes, a little heart-aching no doubt, and Espanola has sunk down into the sea behind the white wake of the ships; and with its fading away the span of active life allotted to this man shuts down, and his powerful opportunities for good or evil are withdrawn.

There was something great and heroic about the Admiral's last voyage. Wind and sea rose up as though to make a last bitter attack upon the man who had disclosed their mysteries and betrayed their secrets. He had hardly cleared the island before the first gale came down upon him and dismasted his ship, so that he was obliged to transfer himself and his son to Bartholomew's caravel and send the disabled vessel back to Espanola. The shouting sea, as though encouraged by this triumph, hurled tempest after tempest upon the one lonely small ship that was staggering on its way to Spain; and the duel between this great seaman and the vast elemental power that he had so often outwitted began in earnest. One little ship, one enfeebled man to be destroyed by the power of the sea: that was the problem, and there were thousands of miles of sea-room, and two months of time to solve it in! Tempest after tempest rose and drove unceasingly against the ship. A mast was sprung and had to be cut away; another, and the woodwork from the forecastles and high stern works had to be stripped and lashed round the crazy mainmast to preserve it from wholesale destruction. Another gale, and the mast had to be shortened, for even reinforced as it was it would not bear the strain; and so crippled, so buffeted, this very small ship leapt and staggered on her way across the Atlantic, keeping her bowsprit pointed to that region of the foamy emptiness where Spain was.

The Admiral lay crippled in his cabin listening to the rush and bubble of the water, feeling the blows and recoils of the unending battle, hearkening anxiously to the straining of the timbers and the vessel's agonised complainings under the pounding of the seas. We do not know what his thoughts were; but we may guess that they looked backward rather than forward, and that often they must have been prayers that the present misery would come somehow or other to an end. Up on deck brother Bartholomew, who has developed some grievous complaint of the jaws and teeth— complaint not known to us more particularly, but dreadful enough from that description—does his duty also, with that heroic manfulness that has marked his whole career; and somewhere in the ship young Ferdinand is sheltering from the sprays and breaking seas, finding his world of adventure grown somewhat gloomy and sordid of late, and feeling that he has now had his fill of the sea . . . . Shut your eyes and let the illusions of time and place fade from you; be with them for a moment on this last voyage; hear that eternal foaming and crashing of great waves, the shrieking of wind in cordage, the cracking and slatting of the sails, the mad lashing of loose ropes; the painful swinging, and climbing up and diving down, and sinking and staggering and helpless strivings of the small ship in the waste of water. The sea is as empty as chaos, nothing for days and weeks but that infinite tumbling surface and heaven of grey storm-clouds; a world of salt surges encircled by horizons of dim foam. Time and place are nothing; the agony and pain of such moments are eternal.

But the two brothers, grim and gigantic in their sea power, subtle as the wind itself in their sea wit, win the battle. Over the thousands of miles of angry surges they urge that small ship towards calm and safety; until one day the sea begins to abate a little, and through the spray and tumult of waters the dim loom of land is seen. The sea falls back disappointed and finally conquered by Christopher Columbus, whose ship, battered, crippled, and strained, comes back out of the wilderness of waters and glides quietly into the smooth harbour of San Lucar, November 7, 1504. There were no guns or bells to greet the Admiral; his only salute was in the thunder of the conquered seas; and he was carried ashore to San Lucar, and thence to Seville, a sick and broken man.

CHAPTER IX

THE LAST DAYS

Columbus, for whom rest and quiet were the first essentials, remained in Seville from November 1504 to May 1505, when he joined the Court at Segovia and afterwards at Salamanca and Valladolid, where he remained till his death in May 1506. During this last period, when all other activities were practically impossible to him, he fell into a state of letter-writing—for the most part long, wearisome complainings and explainings in which he poured out a copious flood of tears and self-pity for the loss of his gold.

It has generally been claimed that Columbus was in bitter penury and want of money, but a close examination of the letters and other documents relating to this time show that in his last days he was not poor in any true sense of the word. He was probably a hundred times richer than any of his ancestors had ever been; he had, money to give and money to spend; the banks honoured his drafts; his credit was apparently indisputable. But compared with the fabulous wealth to which he would by this time have been entitled if his original agreement with the Crown of Spain had been faithfully carried out he was no doubt poor. There is no evidence that he lacked any comfort or alleviation that money could buy; indeed he never had any great craving for the things that money can buy—only for money itself. There must have been many rich people in Spain who would gladly have entertained him in luxury and dignity; but he was not the kind of man to set much store by such things except in so far as they were a decoration and advertisement of his position as a great man. He had set himself to the single task of securing what he called his rights; and in these days of sunset he seems to have been illumined by some glimmer of the early glory of his first inspiration. He wanted the payment of his dues now, not so much for his own enrichment, but as a sign to the world that his great position as Admiral and Viceroy was recognised, so that his dignities and estates might be established and consolidated in a form which he would be able to transmit to his remote posterity.

Since he wrote so copiously and so constantly in these last days, the best picture of his mood and condition is afforded in his letters to his son Diego; letters which, in spite of their infinitely wearisome recapitulation and querulous complaint, should be carefully read by those who wish to keep in touch with the Admiral to the end.

Letter written by CHRISTOPHER COLUMBUS to DON DIEGO, his Son, November 21, 1504.

"VERY DEAR SON,—I received your letter by the courier. You did well in remaining yonder to remedy our affairs somewhat and to employ yourself now in our business. Ever since I came to Castile, the Lord Bishop of Palencia has shown me favour and has desired that I should be honoured. Now he must be entreated that it may please him to occupy himself in remedying my many grievances and in ordering that the agreement and letters of concession which their Highnesses gave me be fulfilled, and that I be indemnified for so many damages. And he may be certain that if their Highnesses do this, their estate and greatness will be multiplied to them in an incredible degree. And it must not appear to him that forty thousand pesos in gold is more than a representation of it; because they might have had a much greater quantity if Satan had not hindered it by impeding my design; for, when I was taken away from the Indies, I was prepared to give them a sum of gold incomparable to forty thousand pesos. I make oath, and this may be for thee alone, that the damage to me in the matter of the concessions their Highnesses have made to me, amounts to ten millions each year, and never can be made good. You see what will be, or is, the injury to their Highnesses in what belongs to them, and they do not perceive it. I write at their disposal and will strive to start yonder. My arrival and the rest is in the hands of our Lord. His mercy is infinite. What is done and is to be done, St. Augustine says is already done before the creation of the world. I write also to these other Lords named in the letter of Diego Mendez. Commend me to their mercy and tell them of my going as I have said above. For certainly I feel great fear, as the cold is so inimical to this, my infirmity, that I may have to remain on the road.

"I was very much pleased to hear the contents of your letter and what the King our Lord said, for which you kissed his royal hands. It is certain that I have served their Highnesses with as much diligence and love as though it had been to gain Paradise, and more, and if I have been at fault in anything it has been because it was impossible or because my knowledge and strength were not sufficient. God, our Lord, in such a case, does not require more from persons than the will.

"At the request of the Treasurer Morales, I left two brothers in the Indies, who are called Porras. The one was captain and the other auditor. Both were without capacity for these positions: and I was confident that they could fill them, because of love for the person who sent them to me. They both became more vain than they had been. I forgave them many incivilities, more than I would do with a relation, and their offences were such that they merited another punishment than a verbal reprimand. Finally they reached such a point that even had I desired, I could not have avoided doing what I did. The records of the case will prove whether I lie or not. They rebelled on the island of Jamaica, at which I was as much astonished as I would be if the sun's rays should cast darkness. I was at the point of death, and they martyrised me with extreme cruelty during five months and without cause. Finally I took them all prisoners, and immediately set them free, except the captain, whom I was bringing as a prisoner to their Highnesses. A petition which they made to me under oath, and which I send you with this letter, will inform you at length in regard to this matter, although the records of the case explain it fully. These records and the Notary are coming on another vessel, which I am expecting from day to day. The Governor in Santo Domingo took this prisoner.—His courtesy constrained him to do this. I had a chapter in my instructions in which their Highnesses ordered all to obey me, and that I should exercise civil and criminal justice over all those who were with me: but this was of no avail with the Governor, who said that it was not understood as applying in his territory. He sent the prisoner to these Lords who have charge of the Indies without inquiry or record or writing. They did not receive him, and both brothers go free. It is not wonderful to me that our Lord punishes. They went there with shameless faces. Such wickedness or such cruel treason were never heard of. I wrote to their Highnesses about this matter in the other letter, and said that it was not right for them to consent to this offence. I also wrote to the Lord Treasurer that I begged him as a favour not to pass sentence on the testimony given by these men until he heard me. Now it will be well for you to remind him of it anew. I do, not know how they dare to go before him with such an undertaking. I have written to him about it again and have sent him the copy of the oath, the same as I send to you and likewise to Doctor Angulo and the Licentiate Zapata. I commend myself to the mercy of all, with the information that my departure yonder will take place in a short time.

"I would be glad to receive a letter from their Highnesses and to know what they order. You must procure such a letter if you see the means of so doing. I also commend myself to the Lord Bishop and to Juan Lopez, with the reminder of illness and of the reward for my services.

"You must read the letters which go with this one in order to act in conformity with what they say. Acknowledge the receipt of his letter to Diego Mendez. I do not write him as he will learn everything from you, and also because my illness prevents it.

"It would be well for Carbajal and Jeronimo—[Jeronimo de Aguero, a landowner in Espanola and a friend of Columbus]—to be at the-Court at this time, and talk of our affairs with these Lords and with the Secretary.

"Done in Seville, November 21.

"Your father who loves you more than himself.

.S.

.S.A.S.

XMY

Xpo FERENS."

"I wrote again to their Highnesses entreating them to order that these people who went with me should be paid, because they are poor and it is three years since they left their homes. The news which they bring is more than extraordinary. They have endured infinite dangers and hardships. I did not wish to rob the country, so as not to cause scandal, because reason advises its being populated, and then gold will be obtained freely without scandal. Speak of this to the Secretary and to the Lord Bishop and to Juan Lopez and to whomever you think it advisable to do so."

The Bishop of Palencia referred to in this letter is probably Bishop Fonseca—probably, because it is known that he did become Bishop of Palencia, although there is a difference of opinion among historians as to whether the date of his translation to that see was before or after this letter. No matter, except that one is glad to think that an old enemy—for Fonseca and Columbus had bitter disagreements over the fitting out of various expeditions—had shown himself friendly at last.

Letter written by CHRISTOPHER COLUMBUS to DON DIEGO, November 28, 1504.

"VERY DEAR SON,—I received your letters of the 15th of this month. It is eight days since I wrote you and sent the letter by a courier. I enclosed unsealed letters to many other persons, in order that you might see them, and having read them, seal and deliver them. Although this illness of mine troubles me greatly, I am preparing for my departure in every way. I would very much like to receive the reply from their Highnesses and wish you might procure it: and also I wish that their Highnesses would provide for the payment of these poor people, who have passed through incredible hardships and have brought them such great news that infinite thanks should be given to God, our Lord, and they should rejoice greatly over it. If I [lie ?] the 'Paralipomenon'—[The Book of Chronicles]—and the Book of Kings and the Antiquities of Josephus, with very many others, will tell what they know of this. I hope in our Lord to depart this coming week, but you must not write less often on that account. I have not heard from Carbajal and Jeronimo. If they are there, commend me to them. The time is such that both Carbajals ought to be at Court, if illness does not prevent them. My regards to Diego Mendez.

"I believe that his truth and efforts will be worth as much as the lies of the Porras brothers. The bearer of this letter is Martin de Gamboa. I am sending by him a letter to Juan Lopez and a letter of credit. Read the letter to Lopez and then give it to him. If you write me, send the letters to Luis de Soria that he may send them wherever I am, because if I go in a litter, I believe it will be by La Plata.—[The old Roman road from Merida to Salamanca.]—May our Lord have you in His holy keeping. Your uncle has been very sick and is now, from trouble with his jaws and his teeth.

"Done in Seville, November 28.

"Your father who loves you more than himself.

.S.

.S.A.S.

XMY

Xpo FERENS."

Bartholomew Columbus and Ferdinand were remaining with Christopher at Seville; Bartholomew probably very nearly as ill as the Admiral, although we do not hear so many complaints about it. At any rate Diego, being ay Court, was the great mainstay of his father; and you can see the sick man sitting there alone with his grievances, and looking to the next generation for help in getting them redressed. Diego, it is to be feared, did not receive these letters with so much patience and attention as he might have shown, nor did he write back to his invalid father with the fulness and regularity which the old man craved. It is a fault common to sons. Those who are sons will know that it does not necessarily imply lack of affection on Diego's part; those who are fathers will realise how much Christopher longed for verbal assurance of interest and affection, even though he did not doubt their reality. News of the serious illness of Queen Isabella had evidently reached Columbus, and was the chief topic of public interest.

Letter written by CHRISTOPHER COLUMBUS to DON DIEGO, his Son, December 1, 1504.

"VERY DEAR SON,—Since I received your letter of November 15 I have heard nothing from you. I wish that you would write me more frequently. I would like to receive a letter from you each hour. Reason must tell you that now I have no other repose. Many couriers come each day, and the news is of such a nature and so abundant that on hearing it all my hair stands on end; it is so contrary to what my soul desires. May it please the Holy Trinity to give health to the Queen, our Lady, that she may settle what has already been placed under discussion. I wrote you by another courier Thursday, eight days ago. The courier must already be on his way back here. I told you in that letter that my departure was certain, but that the hope of my arrival there, according to experience, was very uncertain, because my sickness is so bad, and the cold is so well suited to aggravate it, that I could not well avoid remaining in some inn on the road. The litter and everything were ready. The weather became so violent that it appeared impossible to every one to start when it was getting so bad, and that it was better for so well-known a person as myself to take care of myself and try to regain my health rather than place myself in danger. I told you in those letters what I now say, that you decided well in remaining there (at such a time), and that it was right to commence occupying yourself with our affairs; and reason strongly urges this. It appears to me that a good copy should be made of the chapter of that letter which their Highnesses wrote me where they say they will fulfil their promises to me and will place you in possession of everything: and that this copy should be given to them with another writing telling of my sickness, and that it is now impossible for me to go and kiss their Royal feet and hands, and that the Indies are being lost, and are on fire in a thousand places, and that I have received nothing, and am receiving nothing, from the revenues derived from them, and that no one dares to accept or demand anything there for me, and I am living upon borrowed funds. I spent the money which I got there in bringing those people who went with me back to their homes, for it would be a great burden upon my conscience to have left them there and to have abandoned them. This must be made known to the Lord Bishop of Palencia, in whose favour I have so much confidence, and also to the Lord Chamberlain. I believed that Carbajal and Jeronimo would be there at such a time. Our Lord is there, and He will order everything as He knows it to be best for us.

"Carbajal reached here yesterday. I wished to send him immediately with this same order, but he excused himself profusely, saying that his wife was at the point of death. I shall see that he goes, because he knows a great deal about these affairs. I will also endeavour to have your brother and your uncle go to kiss the hands of Their Highnesses, and give them an account of the voyage if my letters are not sufficient. Take good care of your brother. He has a good disposition, and is no longer a boy. Ten brothers would not be too many for you. I never found better friends to right or to left than my brothers. We must strive to obtain the government of the Indies and then the adjustment of the revenues. I gave you a memorandum which told you what part of them belongs to me. What they gave to Carbajal was nothing and has turned to nothing. Whoever desires to do so takes merchandise there, and so the eighth is nothing, because, without contributing the eighth, I could send to trade there without rendering account or going in company with any one. I said a great many times in the past that the contribution of the eighth would come to nothing. The eighth and the rest belongs to me by reason of the concession which their Highnesses made to me, as set forth in the book of my Privileges, and also the third and the tenth. Of the tenth I received nothing, except the tenth of what their Highnesses receive; and it must be the tenth of all the gold and other things which are found and obtained, in whatever manner it may be, within this Admiralship, and the tenth of all the merchandise which goes and comes from there, after the expenses are deducted. I have already said that in the Book of Privileges the reason for this and for the rest which is before the Tribunal of the Indies here in Seville, is clearly set forth.

"We must strive to obtain a reply to my letter from their Highnesses, and to have them order that these people be paid. I wrote in regard to this subject four days ago, and sent the letter by Martin de Gamboa, and you must have seen the letter of Juan Lopez with your own.

"It is said here that it has been ordered that three or four Bishops of the Indies shall be sent or created, and that this matter is referred to the Lord Bishop of Palencia. After having commended me to his Worship, tell him that I believe it will best serve their Highnesses for me to talk with him before this matter is settled.

"Commend me to Diego Mendez, and show him this letter. My illness permits me to write only at night, because in the daytime my hands are deprived of strength. I believe that a son of Francisco Pinelo will carry this letter. Entertain him well, because he does everything for me that he can, with much love and a cheerful goodwill. The caravel which broke her mast in starting from Santo Domingo has arrived in the Algarves. She brings the records of the case of the Porras brothers. Such ugly things and such grievous cruelty as appear in this matter never were seen. If their Highnesses do not punish it, I do not know who will dare to go out in their service with people.

"To-day is Monday. I will endeavour to have your uncle and brother start to-morrow. Remember to write me very often, and tell Diego Mendez to write at length. Each day messengers go from here yonder. May our Lord have you in His Holy keeping.

"Done in Seville, December 1.

"Your father who loves you as himself.

.S.

.S.A.S.

XMY

Xpo FERENS."

The gout from which the Admiral suffered made riding impossible to him, and he had arranged to have himself carried to Court on a litter when he was able to move. There is a grim and dismal significance in the particular litter that had been chosen: it was no other than the funeral bier which belonged to the Cathedral of Seville and had been built for Cardinal Mendoza. A minute of the Cathedral Chapter records the granting to Columbus of the use of this strange conveyance; but one is glad to think that he ultimately made his journey in a less grim though more humble method. But what are we to think of the taste of a man who would rather travel in a bier, so long as it had been associated with the splendid obsequies of a cardinal, than in the ordinary litter of every-day use? It is but the old passion for state and splendour thus dismally breaking out again.

He speaks of living on borrowed funds and of having devoted all his resources to the payment of his crew; but that may be taken as an exaggeration. He may have borrowed, but the man who can borrow easily from banks cannot be regarded as a poor man. One is nevertheless grateful for these references, since they commemorate the Admiral's unfailing loyalty to those who shared his hardships, and his unwearied efforts to see that they received what was due to them. Pleasant also are the evidences of warm family affection in those simple words of brotherly love, and the affecting advice to Diego that he should love his brother Ferdinand as Christopher loved Bartholomew. It is a pleasant oasis in this dreary, sordid wailing after thirds and tenths and eighths. Good Diego Mendez, that honourable gentleman, was evidently also at Court at this time, honestly striving, we may be sure, to say a good word for the Admiral.

Some time after this letter was written, and before the writing of the next, news reached Seville of the death of Queen Isabella. For ten years her kind heart had been wrung by many sorrows. Her mother had died in 1496; the next year her only son and heir to the crown had followed; and within yet another year had died her favourite daughter, the Queen of Portugal. Her other children were all scattered with the exception of Juana, whose semi-imbecile condition caused her parents an anxiety greater even than that caused by death. As Isabella's life thus closed sombrely in, she

---

applied herself more closely and more narrowly to such pious consolations as were available. News from Flanders of the scandalous scenes between Philip and Juana in the summer of 1504 brought on an illness from which she really never recovered, a kind of feverish distress of mind and body in which her only alleviation was the transaction of such business as was possible for her in the direction of humanity and enlightenment. She still received men of intellect and renown, especially travellers. But she knew that her end was near, and as early as October she had made her will, in which her wishes as to the succession and government of Castile were clearly laid down. There was no mention of Columbus in this will, which afterwards greatly mortified him; but it is possible that the poor Queen had by this time, even against her wish, come to share the opinions of her advisers that the rule of Columbus in the West Indies had not brought the most humane and happy results possible to the people there.

During October and November her life thus beat itself away in a succession of duties faithfully performed, tasks duly finished, preparations for the great change duly made. She died, as she would have wished to die, surrounded by friends who loved and admired her, and fortified by the last rites of the Church for her journey into the unknown. Date, November 26, 1504, in the fifty-fourth year of her age.

Columbus had evidently received the news from a public source, and felt mortified that Diego should not have written him a special letter.

Letter written by CHRISTOPHER COLUMBUS to DON DIEGO, his Son, December 3, 1504.

"VERY DEAR SON,—I wrote you at length day before yesterday and sent it by Francisco Pinelo, and with this letter I send you a very full memorandum. I am very much astonished not to receive a letter from you or from any one else, and this astonishment is shared by all who know me. Every one here has letters, and I, who have more reason to expect them, have none. Great care should be taken about this matter. The memorandum of which I have spoken above says enough, and on this account I do not speak more at length here. Your brother and your uncle and Carbajal are going yonder. You will learn from them what is not said here. May our Lord have you in His Holy keeping.

"Done in Seville, December 3.

"Your father who loves you more than himself.

.S.

.S.A.S.

XMY

Xpo FERENS."

Document of COLUMBUS addressed to his Son, DIEGO, and intended to accompany the preceding letter.

"A memorandum for you, my very dear son, Don Diego, of what occurs to me at the present time which must be done:—The principal thing is, affectionately and with great devotion to commend the soul of the Queen, our Lady, to God. Her life was always Catholic and Holy and ready for all the things of His holy service, and for this reason it must be believed that she is in His holy glory and beyond the desires of this rough and wearisome world. Then the next thing is to be watchful and exert one's self in the service of the King, our Lord, and to strive to keep him from being troubled. His Highness is the head of Christendom. See the proverb which says that when the head aches, all the members ache. So that all good Christians should entreat that he may have long life and health: and those of us who are obliged to serve him more than others must join in this supplication with great earnestness and diligence. This reason prompts me now with my severe illness to write you what I am writing here, that his Highness may dispose matters for his service: and for the better fulfilment I am sending your brother there, who, although he is a child in days, is not a child in understanding; and I am sending your uncle and Carbajal, so that if this, my writing, is not sufficient, they, together with yourself, can furnish verbal evidence. In my opinion there is nothing so necessary for the service of his Highness as the disposition and remedying of the affair of the Indies.

"His Highness must now have there more than 40,000 or 50,000 gold pieces. I learned when I was there that the Governor had no desire to send it to him. It is believed among the other people as well that there will be 150,000 pesos more, and the mines are very rich and productive. Most of the people there are common and ignorant, and care very little for the circumstances. The Governor is very much hated by all of them, and it is to be feared that they may at some time rebel. If this should occur, which God forbid, the remedy for the matter would then be difficult: and so it would be if injustice were used toward them, either here or in other places, with the great fame of the gold. My opinion is that his Highness should investigate this affair quickly and by means of a person who is interested and who can go there with 150 or 200 people well equipped, and remain there until it is well settled and without suspicion, which cannot be done in less than three months: and that an endeavour be made to raise two or three forces there. The gold there is exposed to great risk, as there are very few people to protect it. I say that there is a proverb here which says that the presence of the owner makes the horse fat. Here and wherever I may be, I shall serve their Highnesses with joy, until my soul leaves this body.

"Above I said that his Highness is the head of the Christians, and that it is necessary for him to occupy himself in preserving them and their lands. For this reason people say that he cannot thus provide a good government for all these Indies, and that they are being lost and do not yield a profit, neither are they being handled in a reasonable manner. In my opinion it would serve him to intrust this matter to some one who is distressed over the bad treatment of his subjects.

"I wrote a very long letter to his Highness as soon as I arrived here, fully stating the evils which require a prompt and efficient remedy at once. I have received no reply, nor have I seen any provision made in the matter. Some vessels are detained in San Lucar by the weather. I have told these gentlemen of the Board of Trade that they must order them held until the King, our Lord, makes provision in the matter, either by some person with other people, or by writing. This is very necessary and I know what I say. It is necessary that the authorities should order all the ports searched diligently, to see that no one goes yonder to the Indies without licence. I have already said that there is a great deal of gold collected in straw houses without any means of defence, and there are many disorderly people in the country, and that the Governor is hated, and that little punishment is inflicted and has been inflicted upon those who have committed crimes and have come out with their treasonable conduct approved.

"If his Highness decides to make some provision, it must be done at once, so that these vessels may not be injured.

"I have heard that three Bishops are to be elected and sent to Espanola. If it pleases his Highness to hear me before concluding this matter, I will tell in what manner God our Lord may be well served and his Highness served and satisfied.

"I have given lengthy consideration to the provision for Espanola:"

Yes, the Queen is in His Holy Glory, and beyond the desires of this rough and wearisome world; but we are not; we are still in a world where fifty thousand gold pieces can be of use to us, and where a word spoken in season, even in such a season of darkness, may have its effect with the King. A strange time to talk to the King about gold; and perhaps Diego was wiser and kinder than his father thought in not immediately taking this strange document to King Ferdinand.

Letter written by CHRISTOPHER COLUMBUS to DON DIEGO, his Son, December 13, 1504

"VERY DEAR SON,—It is now eight days since your uncle and your brother and Carbajal left here together, to kiss the royal hands of his Highness, and to give an account of the voyage, and also to aid you in the negotiation of whatever may prove to be necessary there.

"Don Ferdinand took from here 150 ducats to be expended at his discretion. He will have to spend some of it, but he will give you what he has remaining. He also carries a letter of credit for these merchants. You will see that it is very necessary to be careful in dealing with them, because I had trouble there with the Governor, as every one told me that I had there 11,000 or 12,000 castellanos, and I had only 4000. He wished to charge me with things for which I am not indebted, and I, confiding in the promise of their Highnesses, who ordered everything restored to me, decided to leave these charges in the hope of calling him to account for them. If any one has money there, they do not dare ask for it, on account of his haughtiness. I very well know that after my departure he must have received more than 5000 castellanos. If it were possible for you to obtain from his Highness an authoritative letter to the Governor, ordering him to send the money without delay and a full account of what belongs to me, by the person I might send there with my power of attorney, it would be well; because he will not give it in any other manner, neither to my friend Diaz or Velasquez, and they dare not even speak of it to him. Carbajal will very well know how this must be done. Let him see this letter. The 150 ducats which Luis de Soria sent you when I came are paid according to his desire.

"I wrote you at length and sent the letter by Don Ferdinand, also a memorandum. Now that I have thought over the matter further, I say that, since at the time of my departure their Highnesses said over their signature and verbally, that they would give me all that belongs to me, according to my privileges—that the claim for the third or the tenth and eighth mentioned in the memorandum must be relinquished, and instead the chapter of their letter must be shown where they write what I have said, and all that belongs to me must be required, as you have it in writing in the Book of Privileges, in which is also set forth the reason for my receiving the third, eighth, and tenth; as there is always an opportunity to reduce the sum desired by a person, although his Highness says in his letter that he wishes to give me all that belongs to me. Carbajal will understand me very well if he sees this letter, and every one else as well, as it is very clear. I also wrote to his Highness and finally reminded him that he must provide at once for this affair of the Indies, that the people there may not be disturbed, and also reminding him of the promise stated above. You ought to see the letter.

"With this letter I send you another letter of credit for the said merchants. I have already explained to you the reasons why expenses should be moderated. Show your uncle due respect, and treat your brother as an elder brother should treat a younger. You have no other brother, and praised be our Lord, he is such a one as you need very much. He has proved and proves to be very intelligent. Honour Carbajal and Jeronimo and Diego Mendez. Commend me to them all. I do not write them as there is nothing to write and this messenger is in haste. It is frequently rumoured here that the Queen, whom God has, has left an order that I be restored to the possession of the Indies. On arrival, the notary of the fleet will send you the records and the original of the case of the Porras brothers. I have received no news from your uncle and brother since they left. The water has been so high here that the river entered the city.

"If Agostin Italian and Francisco de Grimaldo do not wish to give you the money you need, look for others there who are willing to give it to you. On the arrival here of your signature I will at once pay them all that you have received: for at present there is not a person here by whom I can send you money.

"Done to-day, Friday, December 13, 1504

"Your father who loves you more than himself.

.S.

.S.A.S.

XMY

Xpo FERENS."

Letter written by CHRISTOPHER COLUMBUS to his Son, DON DIEGO, December 21, 1504.

"VERY DEAR SON, The Lord Adelantado and your brother and Carbajal left here sixteen days ago to go to the Court. They have not written me since. Don Ferdinand carried 150 ducats. He must spend what is necessary, and he carries a letter, that the merchants may furnish you with money. I have sent you another letter since, with the endorsement of Francisco de Ribarol, by Zamora, the courier, and told you that if you had made provision for yourself by means of my letter, not to use that of Francisco de Ribarol. I say the same now in regard to another letter which I send you with this one, for Francisco Doria, which letter I send you for greater security that you may not fail to be provided with money. I have already told you how necessary it is to be careful in the expenditure of the money, until their Highnesses give us law and justice. I also told you that I had spent 1200 castellanos in bringing these people to Castile, of which his Highness owes me the greater part, and I wrote him in regard to it asking him to order the account settled.

"If possible I should like to receive letters here each day. I complain of Diego Mendez and of Jeronimo, as they do not write me: and then of the others who do not write when they arrive there. We must strive to learn whether the Queen, whom God has in His keeping, said anything about me in her will, and we must hurry the Lord Bishop of Palencia, who caused the possession of the Indies by their Highnesses and my remaining in Castile, for I was already on my way to leave it. And the Lord Chamberlain of his Highness must also be hurried. If by chance the affair comes to discussion, you must strive to have them see the writing which is in the Book of Privileges, which shows the reason why the third, eighth, and tenth are owing me, as I told you in another letter.

"I have written to the Holy Father in regard to my voyage, as he complained of me because I did not write him. I send you a copy of the letter. I would like to have the King, our Lord, or the Lord Bishop of Palencia see it before I send the letter, in order to avoid false representations.

"Camacho has told a thousand falsehoods about me. To my regret I ordered him arrested. He is in the church. He says that after the Holidays are past, he will go there if he is able. If I owe him, he must show by what reason; for I make oath that I do not know it, nor is it true.

"If without importunity a licence can be procured for me to go on mule-back, I will try to leave for the Court after January, and I will even go without this licence. But haste must be made that the loss of the Indies, which is now imminent, may not take place. May our Lord have you in His keeping.

"Done to-day, December 21.

"Your father who loves you more than himself.

.S.

.S.A.S.

XMY

Xpo FERENS."

"This tenth which they give me is not the tenth which was promised me. The Privileges tell what it is, and there is also due me the tenth of the profit derived from merchandise and from all other things, of which I have received nothing. Carbajal understands me well. Also remind Carbajal to obtain a letter from his Highness for the Governor, directing him to send his accounts and the money I have there, at once. And it would be well that a Repostero of his Highness should go there to receive this money, as there must be a large amount due me. I will strive to have these gentlemen of the Board of Trade send also to say to the Governor that he must send my share together with the gold belonging to their Highnesses. But the remedy for the other matter must not be neglected there on this account. I say that 7000 or 8000 pesos must have passed to my credit there, which sum has been received since I left, besides the other money which was not given to me.

"To my very dear son Don Diego at the Court."

All this struggling for the due payment of eighths and tenths makes wearisome reading, and we need not follow the Admiral into his distinctions between one kind of tenth and another. There is something to be said on his side, it must be remembered; the man had not received what was due to him; and although he was not in actual poverty, his only property in this world consisted of these very thirds and eighths and tenths. But if we are inclined to think poorly of the Admiral for his dismal pertinacity, what are we to think of the people who took advantage of their high position to ignore consistently the just claims made upon them?

There is no end to the Admiral's letter-writing at this time. Fortunately for us his letter to the Pope has been lost, or else we should have to insert it here; and we have had quite enough of his theological stupors. As for the Queen's will, there was no mention of the Admiral in it; and her only reference to the Indies showed that she had begun to realise some of the disasters following his rule there, for the provisions that are concerned with the New World refer exclusively to the treatment of the natives, to whose succour, long after they were past succour, the hand of Isabella was stretched out from the grave. The licence to travel on mule-back which the Admiral asked for was made necessary by a law which had been passed forbidding the use of mules for this purpose throughout Spain. There had been a scarcity of horses for mounting the royal cavalry, and it was thought that the breeding of horses had been neglected on account of the greater cheapness and utility of mules. It was to encourage the use and breeding of horses that an interdict was laid on the use of mules, and only the very highest persons in the land were allowed to employ them.

Letter written by CHRISTOPHER COLUMBUS to his Son, DON DIEGO, December 29, 1504.

"VERY DEAR SON,—I wrote you at length and sent it by Don Ferdinand, who left to go yonder twenty-three days ago to-day, with the Lord Adelantado and Carbajal, from whom I have since heard nothing. Sixteen days ago to-day I wrote you and sent it by Zamora, the courier, and I sent you a letter of credit for these merchants endorsed by Francisco de Ribarol, telling them to give you the money you might ask for. And then, about eight days ago, I sent you by another courier a letter endorsed by Francisco Soria, and these letters are directed to Pantaleon and Agostin Italian, that they may give it to you. And with these letters goes a copy of a letter which I wrote to the Holy Father in regard to the affairs of the Indies, that he might not complain of me any more. I sent this copy for his Highness to see, or the Lord Bishop of Palencia, so as to avoid false representations. The payment of the people who went with me has been delayed. I have provided for them here what I have been able. They are poor and obliged to go in order to earn a living. They decided to go yonder. They have been told here that they will be dealt with as favourably as possible, and this is right, although among them there are some who merit punishment more than favours. This is said of the rebels. I gave these people a letter for the Lord Bishop of Palencia. Read it, and if it is necessary for them to go and petition his Highness, urge your uncle and brother and Carbajal to read it also, so that you can all help them as much as possible. It is right and a work of mercy, for no one ever earned money with so many dangers and hardships and no one has ever rendered such great service as these people. It is said that Camacho and Master Bernal wish to go there—two creatures for whom God works few miracles: but if they go, it will be to do harm rather than good. They can do little because the truth always prevails, as it did in Espanola, from which wicked people by means of falsehoods have prevented any profit being received up to the present time. It is said that this Master Bernal was the beginning of the treason. He was taken and accused of many misdemeanours, for each one of which he deserved to be quartered. At the request of your uncle and of others he was pardoned, on condition that if he ever said the least word against me and my state the pardon should be revoked and he should be under condemnation. I send you a copy of the case in this letter. I send you a legal document about Camacho. For more than eight days he has not left the church on account of his rash statements and falsehoods. He has a will made by Terreros, and other relatives of the latter have another will of more recent date, which renders the first will null, as far as the inheritance is concerned: and I am entreated to enforce the latter will, so that Camacho will be obliged to restore what he has received. I shall order a legal document drawn up and served upon him, because I believe it is a work of mercy to punish him, as he is so unbridled in his speech that some one must punish him without the rod: and it will not be so much against the conscience of the chastiser, and will injure him more. Diego Mendez knows Master Bernal and his works very well. The Governor wished to imprison him at Espanola and left him to my consideration. It is said that he killed two men there with medicines in revenge for something of less account than three beans. I would be glad of the licence to travel on muleback and of a good mule, if they can be obtained without difficulty. Consult all about our affairs, and tell them that I do not write them in particular on account of the great pain I feel when writing. I do not say that they must do the same, but that each one must write me and very often, for I feel great sorrow that all the world should have letters from there each day, and I have nothing, when I have so many people there. Commend me to the Lord Adelantado in his favour, and give my regards to your brother and to all the others.

"Done at Seville, December 29.

"Your father who loves you more than himself.

.S.

.S.A.S.

XMY

Xpo FERENS."

"I say further that if our affairs are to be settled according to conscience, that the chapter of the letter which their Highnesses wrote me when I departed, in which they say they will order you placed in possession, must be shown; and the writing must also be shown which is in the Book of Privileges, which shows how in reason and in justice the third and eighth and the tenth are mine. There will always be opportunity to make reductions from this amount."

Columbus's requests were not all for himself; nothing could be more sincere or generous than the spirit in which he always strove to secure the just payment of his mariners.

Otherwise he is still concerned with the favour shown to those who were treasonable to him. Camacho was still hiding in a church, probably from the wrath of Bartholomew Columbus; but Christopher has more subtle ways of punishment. A legal document, he considers, will be better than a rod; "it will not be so much against the conscience of the chastiser, and will injure him (the chastised) more."

Letter written by CHRISTOPHER COLUMBUS to DON DIEGO, his Son, January 18, 1505.

"VERY DEAR SON,—I wrote you at length by the courier who will arrive there to-day, and sent you a letter for the Lord Chamberlain. I intended to inclose in it a copy of that chapter of the letter from their Highnesses in which they say they will order you placed in possession; but I forgot to do it here. Zamora, the courier, came. I read your letter and also those of your uncle and brother and Carbajal, and felt great pleasure in learning that they had arrived well, as I had been very anxious about them. Diego Mendez will leave here in three or four days with the order of payment prepared. He will take a long statement of everything and I will write to Juan Velasquez. I desire his friendship and service. I believe that he is a very honourable gentleman. If the Lord Bishop of Palencia has come, or comes, tell him how much pleased I have been with his prosperity, and that if I go there I must stop with his Worship even if he does not wish it, and that we must return to our first fraternal love. And that he could not refuse it because my service will force him to have it thus. I said that the letter for the Holy Father was sent that his Worship might see it if he was there, and also the Lord Archbishop of Seville, as the King might not have opportunity to read it. I have already told you that the petition to their Highnesses must be for the fulfilment of what they wrote me about the possession and of the rest which was promised me. I said that this chapter of the letter must be shown them and said that it must not be delayed, and that this is advisable for an infinite number of reasons. His Highness may believe that, however much he gives me, the increase of his exalted dominions and revenue will be in the proportion of 100 to 1, and that there is no comparison between what has been done and what is to be done. The sending of a Bishop to Espanola must be delayed until I speak to his Highness. It must not be as in the other cases when it was thought to mend matters and they were spoiled. There have been some cold days here and they have caused me great fatigue and fatigue me now. Commend me to the favour of the Lord Adelantado. May our Lord guard and bless you and your brother. Give my regards to Carbajal and Jeronimo. Diego Mendez will carry a full pouch there. I believe that the affair of which you wrote can be very easily managed. The vessels from the Indies have not arrived from Lisbon. They brought a great deal of gold, and none for me. So great a mockery was never seen, for I left there 60,000 pesos smelted. His Highness should not allow so great an affair to be ruined, as is now taking place. He now sends to the Governor a new provision. I do not know what it is about. I expect letters each day. Be very careful about expenditures, for it is necessary.

"Done January 18.

"Your father who loves you more than himself.

There is playful reference here to Fonseca, with whom Columbus was evidently now reconciled; and he was to be buttonholed and made to read the Admiral's letter to the Pope. Diego Mendez is about to start, and is to make a "long statement"; and in the meantime the Admiral will write as many long letters as he has time for. Was there no friend at hand, I wonder, with wit enough to tell the Admiral that every word he wrote about his grievances was sealing his doom, so far as the King was concerned? No human being could have endured with patience this continuous heavy firing at long range to which the Admiral subjected his friends at Court; every post that arrived was loaded with a shrapnel of grievances, the dull echo of which must have made the ears of those who heard it echo with weariness. Things were evidently humming in Espanola; large cargoes of negroes had been sent out to take the place of the dead natives, and under the harsh driving of Ovando the mines were producing heavily. The vessels that arrived from the Indies brought a great deal of gold; "but none for me."

Letter written by CHRISTOPHER COLUMBUS to his Son, DON DIEGO, February 5, 1505.

"VERY DEAR SON,—Diego Mendez left here Monday, the 3rd of this month. After his departure I talked with Amerigo Vespucci, the bearer of this letter, who is going yonder, where he is called in regard to matters of navigation. He was always desirous of pleasing me. He is a very honourable man. Fortune has been adverse to him as it has been to many others. His labours have not profited him as much as reason demands. He goes for me, and is very desirous of doing something to benefit me if it is in his power. I do not know of anything in which I can instruct him to my benefit, because I do not know what is wanted of him there. He is going with the determination to do everything for me in his power. See what he can do to profit me there, and strive to have him do it; for he will do everything, and will speak and will place it in operation: and it must all be done secretly so that there may be no suspicion.

"I have told him all that could be told regarding this matter, and have informed him of the payment which has been made to me and is being made. This letter is for the Lord Adelantado also, that he may see how Amerigo Vespucci can be useful, and advise him about it. His Highness may believe that his ships went to the best and richest of the Indies, and if anything remains to be learned more than has been told, I will give the information yonder verbally, because it is impossible to give it in writing. May our Lord have you in his Holy keeping.

"Done in Seville, February 5.

"Your father who loves you more than himself.

This letter has a significance which raises it out of the ruck of this complaining correspondence. Amerigo Vespucci had just returned from his long voyage in the West, when he had navigated along an immense stretch of the coast of America, both north and south, and had laid the foundations of a fame which was, for a time at least, to eclipse that of Columbus. Probably neither of the two men realised it at this interview, or Columbus would hardly have felt so cordially towards the man who was destined to rob him of so much glory. As a matter of fact the practical Spaniards were now judging entirely by results; and a year or two later, when the fame of Columbus had sunk to insignificance, he was merely referred to as the discoverer of certain islands, while Vespucci, who after all had only followed in his lead, was hailed as the discoverer of a great continent. Vespucci has been unjustly blamed for this state of affairs, although he could no more control the public estimate of his services than Columbus could. He was a more practical man than Columbus, and he made a much better impression on really wise and intelligent men; and his discoveries were immediately associated with trade and colonial development, while Columbus had little to show for his discoveries during his lifetime but a handful of gold dust and a few cargoes of slaves. At any rate it was a graceful act on the part of Vespucci, whose star was in the ascendant, to go and seek out the Admiral, whose day was fast verging to night; it was one of those disinterested actions that live and have a value of their own, and that shine out happily amid the surrounding murk and confusion.

Letter signed by CHRISTOPHER COLUMBUS to DON DIEGO, his Son, February 25, 1505.

"VERY DEAR SON,—The Licientiate de Zea is a person whom I desire to honour. He has in his charge two men who are under prosecution at the hands of justice, as shown by the information which is inclosed in this letter. See that Diego Mendez places the said petition with the others, that they may be given to his Highness during Holy Week for pardon. If the pardon is granted, it is well, and if not, look for some other manner of obtaining it. May our Lord have you in His Holy keeping. Done in

Seville, February 25, 1505. I wrote you and sent it by Amerigo Vespucci. See that he sends you the letter unless you have already received it.

"Your father.
        Xpo FERENS.//"

This is the last letter of Columbus known to us otherwise an entirely unimportant document, dealing with the most transient affairs. With it we gladly bring to an end this exposure of a greedy and querulous period, which speaks so eloquently for itself that the less we say and comment on it the better.

In the month of May the Admiral was well enough at last to undertake the journey to Segovia. He travelled on a mule, and was accompanied by his brother Bartholomew and his son Ferdinand. When he reached the Court he found the King civil and outwardly attentive to his recitals, but apparently content with a show of civility and outward attention. Columbus was becoming really a nuisance; that is the melancholy truth. The King had his own affairs to attend to; he was already meditating a second marriage, and thinking of the young bride he was to bring home to the vacant place of Isabella; and the very iteration of Columbus's complaints and demands had made them lose all significance for the King. He waved them aside with polite and empty promises, as people do the demands of importunate children; and finally, to appease the Admiral and to get rid of the intolerable nuisance of his applications, he referred the whole question, first to Archbishop DEA, and then to the body of councillors which had been appointed to interpret Queen Isabella's will. The whole question at issue was whether or not the original agreement with Columbus, which had been made before his discoveries, should be carried out. The King, who had foolishly subscribed to it simply as a matter of form, never believing that anything much could come of it, was determined that it should not be carried out, as it would give Columbus a wealth and power to which no mere subject of a crown was entitled. The Admiral held fast to his privileges; the only thing that he would consent to submit to arbitration was the question of his revenues; but his titles and territorial authorities he absolutely stuck to. Of course the council did exactly what the King had done. They talked about the thing a great deal, but they did nothing. Columbus was an invalid and broken man, who might die any day, and it was obviously to their interest to gain time by discussion and delay—a cruel game for our Christopher, who knew his days on earth to be numbered, and who struggled in that web of time in which mortals try to hurry the events of the present and delay the events of the future. Meanwhile Philip of Austria and his wife Juana, Isabella's daughter, had arrived from Flanders to assume the crown of Castile, which Isabella had bequeathed to them. Columbus saw a chance for himself in this coming change, and he sent Bartholomew as an envoy to greet the new Sovereigns, and to enlist their services on the Admiral's behalf. Bartholomew was very well received, but he was too late to be of use to the Admiral, whom he never saw again; and this is our farewell to Bartholomew, who passes out of our narrative here. He went to Rome after Christopher's death on a mission to the Pope concerning some fresh voyages of discovery; and in 1508 he made, so far as we know, his one excursion into romance, when he assisted at the production of an illegitimate little girl—his only descendant. He returned to Espanola under the governorship of his nephew Diego, and died there in 1514 —stern, valiant, brotherly soul, whose devotion to Christopher must be for ever remembered and honoured with the name of the Admiral.

From Segovia Columbus followed the Court to Salamanca and thence to Valladolid, where his increasing illness kept him a prisoner after the Court had left to greet Philip and Juana. He had been in attendance upon it for nearly a year, and without any results: and now, as his infirmity increased, he turned to the settling of his own affairs, and drawing up of wills and codicils—all very elaborate and precise. In these occupations his worldly affairs were duly rounded off; and on May 19, 1506, having finally ratified a will which he had made in Segovia a year before, in which the descent of his honours was entailed upon Diego and his heirs, or failing him Ferdinand and his heirs, or failing him Bartholomew and his heirs, he turned to the settlement of his soul.

His illness had increased gradually but surely, and he must have known that he was dying. He was not without friends, among them the faithful Diego Mendez, his son Ferdinand, and a few others. His lodging was in a small house in an unimportant street of Valladolid, now called the "Calle de Colon"; the house, .No. 7, still standing, and to be seen by curious eyes. As the end approached, the Admiral, who was being attended by Franciscan monks, had himself clothed in a Franciscan habit; and so, on the 20th May 1506, he lay upon his bed, breathing out his life.

. . . And as strange thoughts
>   Grow with a certain humming in my ears,
>   About the life before I lived this life,
>   And this life too, Popes, Cardinals, and priests,
>   Your tall pale mother with her talking eyes
>   And new-found agate urns fresh as day . . .

. . . we do not know what his thoughts were, as the shadows grew deeper about him, as the sounds of the world, the noises from the sunny street, grew fainter, and the images and sounds of memory clearer and louder. Perhaps as he lay there with closed eyes he remembered things long forgotten, as dying people do; sounds and smells of the Vico Dritto di Ponticelli, and the feel of the hot paving-stones down which his childish feet used to run to the sea; noises of the sea also, the drowning swish of waters and sudden roar of breakers sounding to anxiously strained ears in the still night; bright sunlit pictures of faraway tropical shores, with handsome olive figures glistening in the sun; the sight of strange faces, the sound of strange speech, the smell of a strange land; the glitter of gold; the sudden death-shriek breaking the stillness of some sylvan glade; the sight of blood on the grass . . . The Admiral's face undergoes a change; there is a stir in the room; some one signs to the priest Gaspar, who brings forth his sacred wafer and holy oils and administers the last sacraments. The wrinkled eyelids flutter open, the sea-worn voice feebly frames the responses; the dying eyes are fixed on the crucifix; and—"In manus tuas Domine commendo spiritum meum." The Admiral is dead.

He was in his fifty-sixth year, already an old man in body and mind; and his death went entirely unmarked except by his immediate circle of friends. Even Peter Martyr, who was in Valladolid just before and just after it, and who was writing a series of letters to various correspondents giving all the news of his day, never thought it worth while to mention that Christopher Columbus was dead. His life flickered out in the completest obscurity. It is not even known where he was first buried; but probably it was in the Franciscan convent at Valladolid. This, however, was only a temporary resting-place; and a few years later his body was formally interred in the choir of the monastery of Las Cuevas at Seville, there to lie for thirty years surrounded by continual chauntings. After that it was translated to the cathedral in San Domingo; rested there for 250 years, and then, on the cession of that part of the island to France, the body was removed to Cuba. But the Admiral was by this time nothing but a box of bones and dust, as also were brother Bartholomew and son Diego, and Diego's son, all collected together in that place. There were various examinations of the bone-boxes; one, supposed to be the Admiral's, was taken to Cuba and solemnly buried there; and lately, after the conquest of the island in the Spanish-American War, this box of bones was elaborately conveyed to Seville, where it now rests.

But in the meanwhile the Chapter of the cathedral in San Domingo had made new discoveries and examinations; had found another box of bones, which bore to them authentic signs that the dust it contained was the Admiral's and not his grandson's; and in spite of the Academy of History at Madrid, it is indeed far from unlikely that the Admiral's dust does not lie in Spain or Cuba, but in San Domingo still. Whole books have been written about these boxes of bones; learned societies have argued about them, experts have examined the bones and the boxes with microscopes; and meantime the dust of Columbus, if we take the view that an error was committed in the transference to Cuba, is not even collected all in one box. A sacrilegious official acquired some of it when the boxes were opened, and distributed it among various curiosity-hunters, who have preserved it in caskets of crystal and silver. Thus a bit of him is worn by an American lady in a crystal locket; a pinch of him lies in a glass vial in a New York mansion; other pinches in the Lennox Library, New York, in the Vatican, and in the University of Pavia. In such places, if the Admiral should fail to appear at the first note of their trumpets, must the Angels of the Resurrection make search.

CHAPTER X

THE MAN COLUMBUS

It is not in any leaden box or crystal vase that we must search for the true remains of Christopher Columbus. Through these pages we have traced, so far as has been possible, the course of his life, and followed him in what he did; all of which is but preparation for our search for the true man, and just estimate of what he was. We have seen, dimly, what his youth was; that he came of poor people who were of no importance to the world at large; that he earned his living as a working man; that he became possessed of an Idea; that he fought manfully and diligently until he had realised it; and that then he found himself in a position beyond his powers to deal with, not being a strong enough swimmer to hold his own in the rapid tide of events which he himself had set flowing; and we have seen him sinking at last in that tide, weighed down by the very things for which he had bargained and stipulated. If these pages had been devoted to a critical examination of the historical documents on which his life-story is based we should also have found that he continually told lies about himself, and misrepresented facts when the truth proved inconvenient to him; that he was vain and boastful to a degree that can only excite our compassion. He was naturally and sincerely pious, and drew from his religion much strength and spiritual nourishment; but he was also capable of hypocrisy, and of using the self-same religion as a cloak for his greed and cruelty. What is the final image that remains in our minds of such a man? To answer this question we must examine his life in three dimensions. There was its great outline of rise, zenith, and decline; there was its outward history in minute detail, and its conduct in varying circumstances; and there was the inner life of the man's soul, which was perhaps simpler than some of us think. And first, as to his life as a single thing. It rose in poverty, it reached a brief and dazzling zenith of glory, it set in clouds and darkness; the fame of it suffered a long night of eclipse, from which it was rescued and raised again to a height of glory which unfortunately was in sufficiently founded on fact; and as a reaction from this, it has been in danger of becoming entirely discredited, and the man himself denounced as a fraud. The reason for these surprising changes is that in those fifty-five years granted to Columbus for the making of his life he did not consistently listen to that inner voice which alone can hold a man on any constructive path. He listened to it at intervals, and he drew his inspiration from it; but he shut his ears when it had served him, when it had brought him what he wanted. In his moments of success he guided himself by outward things; and thus he was at one moment a seer and ready to be a martyr, and at the next moment he was an opportunist, watching to see which way the wind would blow, and ready to trim his sails in the necessary direction. Such conduct of a man's life does not make for single light or for true greatness; rather for dim, confused lights, and lofty heights obscured in cloud.

If we examine his life in detail we find this alternating principle of conduct revealed throughout it. He was by nature clever, kind-hearted, rather large-souled, affectionate, and not very honest; all the acts prompted by his nature bear the stamp of these qualities. To them his early years had probably added little except piety, sharp practice, and that uncomfortable sense, often bred amid narrow and poor surroundings, that one must keep a sharp look-out for oneself if one is to get a share of the world's good things. Something in his blood, moreover, craved for dignity and the splendour of high-sounding titles; craved for power also, and the fulfilment of an arrogant pride. All these things were in his Ligurian blood, and he breathed them in with the very air of Genoa. His mind was of the receptive rather than of the constructive kind, and it was probably through those long years spent between sea voyages and brief sojourns with his family in Genoa or Savona that he conceived that vague Idea which, as I have tried to show, formed the impulse of his life during its brief initiative period. Having once received this Idea of discovery and like all other great ideas, it was in the air at the time and was bound to take shape in some human brain—he had all his native and personal qualities to bring to its support. The patience to await its course he had learned from his humble and subordinate life. The ambition to work for great rewards was in his blood and race; and to belief in himself, his curious vein of mystical piety was able to add the support of a ready belief in divine selection. This very time of waiting and endurance of disappointments also helped to cultivate in his character two separate qualities—an endurance or ability to withstand infinite hardship and disappointment; and also a greedy pride that promised itself great rewards for whatever should be endured.

In all active matters Columbus was what we call a lucky man. It was luck that brought him to Guanahani; and throughout his life this element of good luck continually helped him. He was lucky, that is to say, in his relation with inanimate things; but in his relations with men he was almost as consistently unlucky. First of all he was probably a bad judge of men. His humble origin and his lack of education naturally made him distrustful. He trusted people whom he should have regarded with suspicion, and he was suspicious of those whom he ought to have known he could trust. If people pleased him, he elevated them with absurd rapidity to stations far beyond their power to fill, and then wondered that they sometimes turned upon him; if they committed crimes against him, he either sought to regain their favour by forgiving them, or else dogged them with a nagging, sulky resentment, and expected every one else to punish them also. He could manage men if he were in the midst of them; there was something winning as well as commanding about his actual presence, and those who were devoted to him would have served him to the death. But when he was not on the spot all his machineries and affairs went to pieces; he had no true organising ability; no sooner did he take his hand off any affair for which he was responsible than it immediately came to confusion. All these defects are to be attributed to his lack of education and knowledge of the world. Mental discipline is absolutely necessary for a man who would discipline others; and knowledge of the world is essential for one who would successfully deal with men, and distinguish those whom he can from those whom he cannot trust. Defects of this nature, which sometimes seem like flaws in the man's character, may be set down to this one disability—that he was not educated and was not by habit a man of the world.

All his sins of misgovernment, then, may be condoned on the ground that governing is a science, and that Columbus had never learned it. What we do find, however, is that the inner light that had led him across the seas never burned clearly for him again, and was never his guide in the later part of his life. Its radiance was quenched by the gleam of gold; for there is no doubt that Columbus was a victim of that baleful influence which has caused so much misery in this world. He was greedy of gold for himself undoubtedly; but he was still more greedy of it for Spain. It was his ambition to be the means of filling the coffers of the Spanish Sovereigns and so acquiring immense dignity and glory for himself. He believed that gold was in itself a very precious and estimable thing; he knew that masses and candles could be bought for it, and very real spiritual privileges; and as he made blunder after blunder, and saw evil after evil heaping itself on his record in the New World, he became the more eager and frantic to acquire such a treasure of gold that it would wipe out the other evils of his administration. And once involved in that circle, there was no help for him.

The man himself was a simple man; capable, when the whole of his various qualities were directed upon one single thing, of that greatness which is the crown of simplicity. Ambition was the keynote of his life; not an unworthy keynote, by any means, if only the ambition be sound; but one serious defect of Columbus's ambition was that it was retrospective rather than perspective. He may have had, before he sailed from Palos, an ambition to be the discoverer of a New World; but I do not think he had. He believed there were islands or land to be discovered in the West if only he pushed on far enough; and he was ambitious to find them and vindicate his belief. Afterwards, when he had read a little more, and when he conceived the plan of pretending that he had all along meant to discover the Indies and a new road to the East, he acted in accordance with that pretence; he tried to make his acts appear retrospectively as though they had been prompted by a design quite different from that by which they had really been prompted. When he found that his discovery was regarded as a great scientific feat, he made haste to pretend that it had all along been meant as such, and was in fact the outcome of an elaborate scientific theory. In all this there is nothing for praise or admiration. It indicates the presence of moral disease; but fortunately it is functional rather than organic disease. He was right and sound at heart; but he spread his sails too readily to the great winds of popular favour, and the result was instability to himself, and often danger of shipwreck to his soul.

The ultimate test of a man's character is how he behaves in certain circumstances when there is no great audience to watch him, and when there is no sovereign close at hand with bounties and rewards to offer. In a word, what matters most is a man's behaviour, not as an admiral, or a discoverer, or a viceroy, or a courtier, but as a man. In this respect Columbus's character rings true. If he was little on little occasions, he was also great on great occasions. The inner history of his fourth voyage, if we could but know it and could take all the circumstances into account, would probably reveal a degree of heroic endurance that has never been surpassed in the history of mankind. Put him as a man face to face with a difficulty, with nothing but his wits to devise with and his two hands to act with, and he is never found wanting. And that is the kind of man of whom discoverers are made. The mere mathematician may work out the facts with the greatest accuracy and prove the existence of land at a certain point; but there is great danger that he may be knocked down by a club on his first landing on the beach, and never bring home any news of his discovery. The great courtier may do well for himself and keep smooth and politic relations with kings; the great administrator may found a wonderful colony; but it is the man with the wits and the hands, and some bigness of heart to tide him over daunting passages, that wins through the first elementary risks of any great discovery. Properly considered, Columbus's fame should rest simply on the answer to the single question, "Did he discover new lands as he said he would?" That was the greatest thing he could do, and the fact that he failed to do a great many other things afterwards, failed the more conspicuously because his attempts were so conspicuous, should have no effect on our estimate of his achievement. The fame of it could no more be destroyed by himself than it can be destroyed by us.

True understanding of a man and estimate of his character can only be arrived at by methods at once more comprehensive and more subtle than those commonly employed among men. Everything that he sees, does, and suffers has its influence on the moulding of his character; and he must be considered in relation to his physical environment, no less than to his race and ancestry. Christopher Columbus spent a great part of his active life on the sea; it was sea-life which inspired him with his great

Idea, it was by the conquest of the sea that he realised it; it was on the sea that all his real triumphs over circumstance and his own weaker self were won. The influences at work upon a man whose life is spent on the sea are as different from those at work upon one who lives on the fields as the environment of a gannet is different from the environment of a skylark: and yet how often do we really attempt to make due allowance for this great factor and try to estimate the extent of its moulding influence?

To live within sound or sight of the sea is to be conscious of a voice or countenance that holds you in unyielding bonds. The voice, being continuous, creeps into the very pulses and becomes part of the pervading sound or silence of a man's environment; and the face, although it never regards him, holds him with its changes and occupies his mind with its everlasting riddle. Its profound inattention to man is part of its power over his imagination; for although it is so absorbed and busy, and has regard for sun and stars and a melancholy frowning concentration upon the foot of cliffs, it is never face to face with man: he can never come within the focus of its great glancing vision. It is somewhere beyond time and space that the mighty perspective of those focal rays comes to its point; and they are so wide and eternal in their sweep that we should find their end, could we but trace them, in a condition far different from that in which our finite views and ethics have place. In the man who lives much on the sea we always find, if he be articulate, something of the dreamer and the mystic; that very condition of mind, indeed, which we have traced in Columbus, which sometimes led him to such heights, and sometimes brought him to such variance with the human code.

A face that will not look upon you can never give up its secret to you; and the face of the sea is like the face of a picture or a statue round which you may circle, looking at it from this point and from that, but whose regard is fixed on something beyond and invisible to you; or it is like the face of a person well known to you in life, a face which you often see in various surroundings, from different angles, now unconscious, now in animated and smiling intercourse with some one else, but which never turns upon you the light of friendly knowledge and recognition; in a word, it is unconscious of you, like all elemental things. In the legend of the Creation it is written that when God saw the gathering together of the waters which he called the Seas, he saw that it was good; and he perhaps had the right to say so. But the man who uses the sea and whose life's pathway is laid on its unstable surface can hardly sum up his impressions of it so simply as to say that it is good. It is indeed to him neither good nor bad; it is utterly beyond and outside all he knows or invents of good and bad, and can never have any concern with his good or his bad. It remains the pathway and territory of powers and mysteries, thoughts and energies on a gigantic and elemental scale; and that is why the mind of man can never grapple with the unconsciousness of the sea or his eye meet its eye. Yet it is the mariner's chief associate, whether as adversary or as ally; his attitude to things outside himself is beyond all doubt influenced by his attitude towards it; and a true comprehension of the man Columbus must include a recognition of this constant influence on him, and of whatever effect lifelong association with so profound and mysterious an element may have had on his conduct in the world of men. Better than many documents as an aid to our understanding of him would be intimate association with the sea, and prolonged contemplation of that face with which he was so familiar. We can never know the heart of it, but we can at least look upon the face, turned from us though it is, upon which he looked. Cloud shadows following a shimmer of sunlit ripples; lines and runes traced on the surface of a blank calm; salt laughter of purple furrows with the foam whipping off them; tides and eddies, whirls, overfalls, ripples, breakers, seas mountains high-they are but movements and changing expressions on an eternal countenance that once held his gaze and wonder, as it will always hold the gaze and wonder of those who follow the sea.

So much of the man Christopher Columbus, who once was and no longer is; perished, to the last bone and fibre of him, off the face of the earth, and living now only by virtue of such truth as there was in him; who once manfully, according to the light that he had, bore Christ on his shoulders across stormy seas, and found him often, in that dim light, a heavy and troublesome burden; who dropped light and burden together on the shores of his discovery, and set going in that place of peace such a conflagration as mankind is not likely to see again for many a generation, if indeed ever again, in this much-tortured world, such ancient peace find place.

The End

www.ingramcontent.com/pod-product-compliance
Lightning Source LLC
Chambersburg PA
CBHW060008300526
45794CB00003B/1139